Phoenix Rising

Ridz.S

BookLeaf Publishing

India | USA | UK

1. The Weight Of Doubt

The way you wear oversized clothes to hide your body,
The way you keep your hair down to hide some of your
face,
The way you cover your face when you cry to hide your
damp eyes,
The way you apply concealer to hide your scars,
The way you put your hand on your mouth when you
laugh to hide your teeth,
The way you quickly say "I'm fine" to hide your feelings,
The way you avoid eye contact to hide your soul,
The way you avoid truly talking to people to hide your
own damn self,
The way you write 'you' in your poetry instead of 'I' to
not feel attacked.

2. Promises Unkept

Forever is just an illusion or a lie?
One promises of forever,
But guess what- promises are meant to be broken.
Broken promises,
Shattered trust,
Soul crushed.
Hope is lost with each promise broken.
Consumed in pain,
Drowned in self-hate,
Thinking what had gone wrong?
Time won't change,
The wound won't heal,
Trust won't be whole.
In the name of love people deceive,
Turning a carefree soul to cold-hearted stone.

3. Destiny?

Is it God's will,
Or do we write it ourselves by the choices we make?
If it is fixed what is about to come,
Why do we dwell on things we can't change?
If everything comes to an end,
What's the point to begin in the first place?
Is it worth all the trouble,
The pain of attachment and a lifetime of sleepless nights?

4. Doubt's Dark Loop

Too early to be this mature,
Trying to know what is wrong?
Afraid I'll hurt you all or,
Bring ominous hazards to all.
I've got many faults,
Of some where I'm at fault
Being naive and a people-pleaser,
A disastrous combination.
It demolished what I built up,
In the cruellest way of one's imagination.
Does history repeat at all?
Or Am I truly at fault?

5. Inevitable Dawn

The agonizing urge to let yourself get drift
In the deep abyss of darkness.
Urge to let the blood seep out of the nerve consuming
mere pulse.
What does one get by hoping for an inevitable action!?
Yet one still hopes with the first ray of sunshine and gets
it broken by the time of moonlighting.
The wait for a miracle equals to wait of a lifetime,
Yet my heart whispers maybe today's right and luck is by
our side...

6. Thorny Bushes

The void in eyes where once used to be emotions, love
and care.
Sweet dreams are replaced by worse nightmares.
The person who radiated warmth and care turned cold
and ruthless.
Haunted by reality, escapism in books.
Either no one has the humanity to notice,
Or the act I put on is Oscar-winning.
Where once used to be a garden filled with flowers
turned out to be thorny bushes,
Either you bleed or stay away.
The feeling of hollowness seeps into my nerves, and I
can't help but sit there without any action.
The soul like mine isn't meant to be loved,
It's meant to stay far away as it ruins everything it
touches!

7. The Labyrinth of Self

You may think all of this is not real,
But I know that's not how you feel,
You just think that's easier to believe,
But by doing that you deceive.
How could you let it get that far?
You tell everyone you're okay,
But we both know the lies in what you say!
You act like you don't care,
But in reality, you fear.
You fear the path that you've chosen,
With your heartbroken.
You fear the thought of letting anyone in,
Cause you fear they will see your sins.
You lock yourself away from everything,
Fearing the disasters it might bring.
You hurt yourself slowly,
Destroy yourself unknowingly,
Give your trust to the god,
But still afraid to see the world.

Why do you Cause yourself so much pain?
Your body and soul are drained...

8. The Fall and the Rise

Sometimes it takes a good fall,
To know where you stand,
In the darkness of self-doubt's hall.

Losing myself, inside my head,
Hurting myself, in the aftermath dread,
Flashbacks striking, like a fatal thread.

The memories one doesn't wish to recall,
Keep recurring, haunting through it all,
For which one desperately seeks out, yet can't define.

The labyrinth of memories continues its torment,
A maze with no escape, no respite, no consent,
Crying speaks emotions that are beyond words,
It inaudibly conveys what lips couldn't utter, nor heard.

But in the silence, a voice starts to rise,
A phoenix from the ashes, with tears in its eyes,
It whispers of strength, of resilience born,

From the depths of pain, a new path is sworn.

The fall was hard, but it's where I stand,
With scars that tell a story, of a soul that's been planned,
To rise again, to heal, to mend,
To find the strength, that lies within, to transcend.

9. Amnesia

Hey Amnesia, be my best friend,
Help me forget, till the very end,
The memories that haunt me, night and day,
The scars that refuse to fade away.

The pain I've endured, the tears I've cried,
The whispers of doubt, that echo inside,
The shadows that follow, wherever I roam,
The weight of memories, that I've made my home.

Forgetfulness, be my solace, my guide,
Help me erase, the lines that won't subside,
The ache of longing, the sting of regret,
The memories that linger, and won't forget.

But alas, Amnesia, you're hard to find,
The memories persist, like a nagging mind,
They resurface, like a tide that's strong,
And I'm left to face, the pain that's been wrong.

Hey Amnesia, if you're listening, please stay,
Be my companion, through these endless days,
Help me forget, and find some peace,
And maybe, just maybe, my heart will release.

10. The Battle Within

I'm drowning in doubts, yet yearning to breathe
A fragile soul, with a heart that beats
Fear of losing, what I've yet to gain
A Paradox of hope, in a sea of pain

I'm searching for solace, in chaotic nights
A desperate quest, for fleeting lights
Self-worth questioned, with every fall
Yet, I rise again, against it all

I'm torn between darkness,
and a glimmer of light,
A battle within, that's my constant fight
Doubts whisper lies, but hope speaks true
I'm lost and found, in this endless pursue.

11. Solace in Shadows

In anxious shadows, I find my home
A comfort in darkness, where fears are known
The whispers of worry, a familiar hum
A solace in solitude, where I am undone

The darkness wraps me, like a shroud of night
A place to hide, from the world's harsh light
The anxiety's grip, a paradoxical peace
A sense of calm, in the chaos that I release

In this quiet turmoil, I find a strange reprieve
A solace in the shadows, where I can breathe
The anxious thoughts, a morbid serenity
A comfort in the darkness, that's my reality

I'll hold on to the shadows, that bring me peace
A solace in the night, where my heart can cease
From the world's loud din, and its judging gaze
I'll find my comfort, in the darkness' quiet ways

12. A Paradox of Love

Under rainfall's melancholy refrain,
I find a solace, in the tears I've gained,
The droplets on my skin, a bittersweet touch,
Washing away doubts, but not the pain so much.

The rain whispers secrets, of peace and rest,
But my heart's a maze, where love's unrest,
The world outside fades, as I step inside,
The rhythmic beat, my chaotic mind.

In rain-kissed moments, I find a fleeting peace,
A moment's calm, from the turmoil that won't cease,
The rain's gentle voice, a soothing balm,
For the self-doubt, that often fuels my shame.

The rain's symphony, a harmony divine,
Echoes the chaos, that's locked inside my mind,
Yet, in its rhythm, I find a melancholy nest,
A refuge from the world, where I'm not my best.

In the rain's embrace, I find a love so true,
A love for the rain, that washes over me anew,
The rain's gentle touch, a healing art,
For the wounds within, that slowly start to scar and part.

I love the rain, but not myself, it seems,
A paradox of love, in the midst of my dreams,
The rain's solace, a temporary reprieve,
From the self-doubt, that my heart can't leave.

13. Hollow Space

Heart racing darkness, words lost in silence,
Emotions suffocating, a storm I can't define,
Fear's heavy chains, binding me tight,
A world outside fading, in the dark of night.

In this hollow space, I'm lost and alone,
The weight of feelings, I struggle to call my own,
A silent scream, that echoes in my head,
A turmoil brewing, that threatens to break instead.

14. Phoenix Born

In a world of facades, we hide our pain,
Behind masks of smiles, and a carefully crafted game,
The weight of expectations, crushes our soul,
As we struggle to find, our true self's role.

The whispers of doubt, echo through our mind,
A constant reminder, of our flaws left behind,
The curated perfection, of social media's stage,
A comparison trap, that turns our hearts to cage.

Tears fall like rain, in the silence of night,
As we grapple with emotions, that we can't ignite,
The search for identity, a journey so unsure,
A path unwinding, through the darkness we're forced to
endure.

The pressure to conform, to fit the mold,
The stress of pleasing, those who never grow old,
The fear of failure, a shadow that looms near,
A constant reminder, of our deepest fear.

Yet, in this darkness, we search for the light,
A glimmer of hope, that guides us through the night,
We yearn for connection, for a listening ear,
For someone to understand, the tears we've shed, the
fears we've held dear.

But from the ashes, we rise, like phoenix born,
Our scars a testament, to the battles we've sworn,
We learn to face our fears, to shatter the chains,
And find our strength, in the heart's deepest pains.

We emerge, like dawn, after a long, dark night,
Our voices whispering, a newfound strength and light,
We rise, no longer, bound by doubt and fear,
But stand, as warriors, with hearts that persevere.

15. Hope's Cruel Whisper

Hope's cruel whisper, a fleeting light,
In darkness's grasp, a fragile sight,
A promise of dawn, after endless night,
Yet shadows linger, a haunting sight.

Hope's gentle touch, a bittersweet reprieve,
A moment's peace, before the pain we leave,
A respite from torment, a calm before the storm,
A fragile haven, where heartache forms.

In this delicate dance, between hope and despair,
We cling to promises, of a brighter air,
But shadows creep, and doubts arise,
And hope's sweet whisper, becomes a distant sigh.

Still, we hold on, to this fleeting light,
A beacon in darkness, a guiding sight,
For in its gentle warmth, we find a way,
To face the shadows, and seize the day.

16. Melancholy Wisdom

Lessons learned, in youthful pain,
A melancholy wisdom, that refuses to wane,
The weight of experience, that shapes my soul,
A premature aging, that makes me whole.

In the fire of trials, I've been refined,
A fragile strength, that's been defined,
The tears I've cried, the scars I've borne,
Have taught me lessons, that I'll forever mourn.

The naivety's gone, the innocence lost,
Replaced by a wisdom, that's been crossed,
With every step, I've learned to tread,
A path of self-discovery, where shadows are fed.

Yet, in this melancholy, I find a peace,
A sense of acceptance, that the world's release,
A knowledge that life's not always kind,
But in its harshness, I've found a strength to find.

17. Echoes of Absence

In empty halls, I search for you,
A silence that echoes, a heart that's blue,
A family member, a loved one's face,
Lost to the shadows, a distant place.

Overthinking minds, a maze of fears,
What ifs and maybes, through sleepless tears,
The weight of uncertainty, a burden to bear,
The thought of never seeing you again, a constant care.

Memories linger, of laughter and of tears,
Of moments shared, and joyous years,
But now, in absence, I'm left to grieve,
A longing that gnaws, a heart that can't breathe.

In this darkness, I cling to hope,
A glimmer of light, a promise to cope,
That somehow, someway, we'll find our way,
And the lost ones, will return to stay.

Until then, I'll hold on to the past,
And cherish the memories, that will forever last,
And though fear may grip, and doubts may rise,
My love for you, will never never die

18. The Other Side of Growing Up

I once rushed time, with impatient heart,
Longing to grow up, to play my part,
To leave behind, the childish ways,
And seize the world, in adult gaze.

But now, I've grown, and wisdom's gained,
I find myself, in a world restrained,
The freedom's lost, the laughter's rare,
And adulthood's weight, I can hardly bear.

I yearn for childhood's simple delight,
For carefree days, and starry nights,
For innocent and wonder's gaze,
For a world untroubled, in joyful haze.

The responsibilities, the stress, the grind,
Have taken toll, on my weary mind,
I long to shed, the burdens I've borne,
And run wild, with childhood's untamed form.

But time keeps moving, and I'm stuck in place,
A prisoner of age, and adult pace,
I dream of recapturing, the joy of youth,
But it's lost forever, in time's unyielding truth.

19. Behind the Masks

In fragile frames, we hide our pain,
Behind masks of smiles, and weighty chains,
Eating disorders creep, like silent thieves,
Stealing self-love, and youthful beliefs.

Peer pressure whispers, a toxic spell,
"Fit in conform, and all will be well",
But in the mirror, a distorted view,
A reflection of self-doubt, forever true.

Adolescence, a maze of conflicting desires,
To fit in, yet stand out, amidst burning fires,
The struggle to belong, to be accepted too,
A delicate balance, we're forever pursuing anew.

Yet, in this darkness, a glimmer of light,
A chance to break free, from the endless fight,
To find our voice, our strength, our way,
To shatter the chains, of societal sway.

But the journey's long, the road is steep,
And setbacks await, in the shadows we keep,
Still, we hold on, to the hope we've found,
That someday, we'll rise, and our true selves resound.

20. Chill of Isolation

Alone in crowds, I stand apart,
A stranger to hearts, a distant start,
The city's noise, a hollow sound,
Echoes of silence, all around.

In isolation's chill, I search for light,
A connection true, a guiding sight,
But shadows loom, and darkness falls,
And I'm left with emptiness hollow calls.

21. The Edge of Transformation

I'm standing at the edge, of a fading light,
A version of myself, that's lost its fight,
The eyes that shone bright, now dim with pain,
The heart that once beat strong, now weak and vain.

I'm saying goodbye, to the ghosts of my past,
The shadows that haunted, the love that didn't last,
The dreams that were crushed, the hopes that were high,
The person I thought I'd be, now goodbye.

In this farewell, I feel a deep sorrow,
A grief for the loss, of a part of tomorrow,
The memories we made, the laughter and the tears,
All fading away, like autumn's disappearing years.

But as I let go, of this worn-out skin,
I feel a glimmer, of a new self within,
A chance to rise, from the ashes of pain,
To find a new voice, a new heart that can sustain.

So I'll bid farewell, to this version of me,
And welcome the new, with its uncertainty,
For in the unknown, lies a chance to grow,
To find a new purpose, a new way to glow.

In this goodbye, I find a glimmer of peace,
A sense of release, from the weight I've released,
I'm stepping into, a brighter light,
A new chapter unfolds, a new story takes flight.

Made with ❤ on the BookLeaf Publishing Platform
www.bookleafpub.in
www.bookleafpub.com

Dedication

For the fragments of my thoughts, and for those who've ever felt the weight of their own overthinking.

Preface

There's a storm that brews quietly in the minds of many —unseen, unheard, but deeply felt. ***Phoenix's Rise*** was born from that very storm.

This collection is a mirror of inner thoughts, late-night spirals, and the kind of overthinking that turns silence into noise. It's for the questions that don't have answers, the pain that doesn't always show, and the strength that builds quietly in the background. These poems speak from the heart of adolescence—a time when everything feels both too much and not enough.

Teenage years can be a battlefield of identity, emotion, and expectation. Every poem here is a fragment of that experience, drawn from raw reflection, quiet battles, and a yearning to be understood. But amidst the chaos, there's growth. And just like the phoenix, rising from its own ashes, there's hope—burning quietly, ready to soar.

This book isn't here to solve your problems. It's here to sit with you in them, speak to the parts of you that feel unheard, and maybe, just maybe, help you find your own rise.

-Ridz.S

Acknowledgements

Writing **Phoenix's Rise** has been more than just putting words on paper—it's been a journey through the loudest corners of a quiet mind. These poems come from moments of confusion, vulnerability, and reflection, and they would never have seen the light without the support of some incredible people.

To everyone who ever listened without judgment, thank you.

Your patience helped me understand the value of being heard.

To my friends who stuck around during the silent days, the overthinking spirals, and the messy emotions—your presence was everything, even when I didn't know how to say it.

To the readers, especially those still finding their way through the chaos of teenage years—this is for you. I hope you find pieces of yourself in these pages, and more than that, I hope you feel less alone.

And lastly, to my past self, who felt too much and said too little—thank you for holding on long enough to let this story rise.

With all my heart,

Ridz.S